MW00528351

A little Book of Poetry
for when night seems dark

Kathi Burg
Illustrations by Kayla Phan

RESOURCE *Publications* • Eugene, Oregon

A gift for:

_____

From:

_____

A LITTLE BOOK OF POETRY
For When Night Seems Dark

Wipf & Stock
An Imprint of Wipf and Stock Publishers
199 W. 8th Ave., Suite 3
Eugene, OR 97401

www.wipfandstock.com

PAPERBACK ISBN: 978-1-7252-7585-0
HARDCOVER ISBN: 978-1-7252-7586-7
EBOOK ISBN: 978-1-7252-7587-4

Illustrations by Kayla Phan
Edited by Eileen Inneken

For anyone who has ever walked in darkness and felt they had no light.

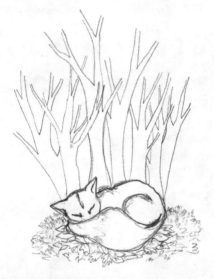

"Let the one who walks in the dark, who has no light, trust in the name of the Lord and rely on their God."
~ Isaiah 50:10

Our Age Of Grayness

The dust is a must
the problem is just
that wrinkles and rust . . .
When the oil can can't
When shall becomes shan't
When our cartilage wears,
and pain-free disappears
When gray becomes white
and feeble, our might
And read, we must
with a much brighter light
Like lettuce, we wilt
Like colors, we fade
Like rainbows, appear
and quick, fade away
Our shell becomes fragile
Our time here is less
But forsaken, we're not
in our age of grayness
To Him be the glory
Who's made us His own
Who made all our joints,

and sinew, and bone
and Who knows where we'll rest
when it's time to go home
To Him be the glory
since orphans, we're not
Since Jesus, He came
and our freedom, He bought
Be cut off from God, anymore?
We cannot
So when tears, they are torn
and blurs, they are blurry
When bruises, they bruise
and muscles don't hurry
When sounds are not sounding
When remembers are less
Be still in the Father
Who fathers us best

"Even to your old age and gray hairs I am he, I am he
who will sustain you. I have made you and I will carry you;
I will sustain you and I will rescue you."
~ Isaiah 46:4

Better Land

I see Him in the rays of sun
that cast a warm, pink glow
I find Him in the crispy cold
that chills my face and toes

I see Him in the melty blues
in lakes below the trees
Where mountains shoot from land to sky
and gift us snowy peaks

He formed the creatures and the moon
He put the stars in place
He grows the seedling from the earth,
moves wind across my face

He's here, and knows your every thought
the things you've always kept
safe, away from diggers deep
where with folded wings, you wept

To restless hearts, He gives new hope
and reaches out a Hand
As we leave our burdens there
and move to better land

"In his hand are the depths of the earth,
and the mountain peaks belong to him."
~ Psalm 95:4

4

When Crawl Became Climb

I thought it just me
weeping aloud
Filling the room
with water and cloud
'Til His voice, I felt
echoing mine
Gave strength to my soul
and crawl became climb

" . . . but those who hope in the Lord will renew their strength.
They will soar on wings like eagles; they will run and not
grow weary, they will walk and not faint."
~ Isaiah 40:31

Bountiful God

When the need was great
and the travel, a climb
When the burden was heavy
and the mountain was high
I looked to the ground
and He showed me the sky . . .

Great Father, my Lord, King of kings
I pray that You'll save me from trivial things
That my heart will be widened,
my vision enlarged
That my soul will find refuge
in the place of You Are

I pray I'll forgive
and learn to re-start
When I want to give up
or break cleanly apart
Bountiful God, please give me release
from the things not of You,
from the parting of peace

"Do not be anxious about anything, but in every situation, by prayer and petition, with thanksgiving, present your requests to God."
~ Philippians 4:6

Hearts In Pieces

Was just me and a book
in my small kitchen nook
when the sun cast a ray, over me, as I shook
Light turned to dark,
hearts were in mourning
and suddenly, thoughts of loss-without-warning

Stories emerged of special lives,
Teachers and nurses, and husbands and wives
Of heroic deeds, and self-sacrifice
Of those who passed, and of those who survived

To the mothers and brothers and sisters and daughters
The spouses, grandparents, grandchildren, sons, fathers
The nephews, the friends, the cousins, the nieces
to all those affected, whose hearts are in pieces

When the sun comes up, we wake with you
we mourn your loss, and ache with you
Pray comfort, you can take with you
know the stories of courage
grew our hearts too

"*The Lord is close to the brokenhearted and saves those who are crushed in spirit.*"
~ *Psalms 34:18*

Heaven

The horizon seemed to speak
to tell me that the line
I saw drawn at its edge
was only to remind

That as sea continues on
stretching from that spot
and places teem with life
that eye would claim, did not

So, life continues still
for those we can't behold
and take our place, we will
among that bless-ed fold

Something meant for all
when turn to Him, we do
An all-inclusive call
not for a chosen few

He said that he did send
His Son not to condemn
but save through Him, He would
an estranged world of men

So call to Him at night
need Him in the dark
tell Him where you stand
with faint or solid heart

He hears each voice that sounds
the whisper and the scream
the shout that fills the air
the fright that fills our dreams

So, know that there is peace
and life beyond this shore
We take His hand, and with each step
renew our hope once more

*"For God did not send his Son into the world to condemn
the world, but to save the world through him."
~ John 3:17*

Tired Feet

I keep crying to You, but it's silent
You must be letting me grow
The only way to find my way
is to walk this path alone?

The Bible says You are my Shield,
My strong Rock and my Peace
So why do I, the labored sigh,
and walk with such tired feet

*"My flesh and my heart may fail, but God is the strength
of my heart and my portion forever."*
~ Psalms 73:26

14

Every Single Tear

She says,
"God wasn't there during the difficult times,"
and I didn't live hers, so it throws me
I look beyond, around, behind
to lock hearts with the One Who grows me

I know other souls in tragic times
saw Jesus standing there
When in dark places,
where no light shined,
they felt Him ever near

It was the sparkle on the water,
the eyes where scales fell
the near death and, "I saw Him!"
a lit up prison cell

So why did she not see You
It troubles me to hear
I know that with her, You were
cupped every single tear

"Where can I go from your Spirit? Where can I flee from
your presence? If I go up to the heavens, you are there;
If I make my bed in the depths, you are there."
~ Psalm 139:7-8

Guts Or Grace

Why does the rain fall so hard
and must it fall in this place
Am I equipped to let it fall
I haven't the guts or the grace

"My soul is weary with sorrow;
strengthen me according to your word."
~ Psalm 119:28

A Sleep

"I'm sorry," can move you to tears,
when the loss is fresh and deep
When you haven't mourned enough,
When it's only been a sleep . . .

*"If I say, 'Surely the darkness will hide me
and the light become night around me,' even the
darkness will not be dark to you . . . "*
~ Psalm 139:11-12

Just Him And You

You will not go with me
when I leave this place
It will only be me and my Maker
When I come to the end,
if I'm frightened old friend
Don't think of Him as a taker

Look up, old friend,
when all seems down
Look past, beyond, away, around
and straight into the face of Him
Who made you from the dust, and when
You come to your departure, then . . .
It's Him and you, and you and Him
Just Him and you, and you and Him

"My Father's house has many rooms; if that were not so,
would I have told you that I am going there to prepare a place for you?
And if I go and prepare a place for you, I will come back
and take you to be with me that you also may be where I am."
~ John 14:2-3

Mighty Realm Of Yours

At night I find a place to hide
amongst Your rocky shores
And though I'm lonely, I'll survive
these mighty waves of Yours

Each cut or scrape will heal in time
reality will never drown me
Any bruises or wounds I'll accept as mine
and let Your high tides rise around me

There's beauty in every sea
There's gold in every ocean
And as abundant are my dreams,
so is my devotion

In the morning I awaken
amongst Your rocky shores
Only to find You've protected me
in this mighty realm of Yours

"*Have mercy on me, my God, have mercy on me,
for in you I take refuge. I will take refuge in the shadow
of your wings until the disaster has passed.*"
~ **Psalm 57:1**

Seed To Stalk

I saw you shoot, from soil to sky
So little I knew, of the you still inside
That one day you'd flower,
that your stalks would reach high,
so little I knew, of your special design

I saw you flourish, then one day you stopped
Your pieces changed color
'til some parts, they dropped
The earth below you, seemed hard as a rock
then suddenly life, in a place it was not

I saw you move, as soon as you knew
that you had a home, and quickly you grew
almost out of the pot you came home in, it's true
And the more that you grew, the more beautiful you

It's from God, is it not?
You, from seed to stalk?
The flowers that bloom,
and the new life in spots?
The reason we grow almost out of our pots?
'Cause we now know Home,
with His life, has been bought

*"I know that my redeemer lives, and that in the end
he will stand on the earth."*
~ Job 19:25

Between The Miracles

They happen every day, I'm told
We just don't always see them
In everyday life, in our routine and haste,
we often think we dream them

But if we open our eyes
to little surprises
they become no surprise at all
And the towering walls,
which obstructed our view
soon begin to fall

But what happens between the miracles
when I'm seeing gray, instead of blue
And I find myself waiting
for the next ray of light
to burst in, and come shining through?

Miracles extend
far beyond the mending of the flesh
and reach into the heart of man
To heal the woundedness

"He heals the brokenhearted and binds up their wounds."
~ Psalm 147:3

A Part Of The Letting Go

This world could have been black and white
but is filled with greens and blues
And a God who says,
it's not what you give
but the love behind the do

And who would have thought that music
would be such a delight to the soul
Where the ear can hear the falling tear
and the heart be filled to full

Sometimes I break
and a part of me leaves
for a place I'll never know
But maybe the emptying out is, indeed
A part of the letting go

"Every good and perfect gift is from above,
coming down from the Father of the heavenly lights,
who does not change like shifting shadows."
~ James 1:17

30

Whose Hands

I am the toy upon the shelf
with dust on every surface
Children play in front of me
and no longer see my purpose

My smile is painted on
and tears fall down my middle
It's the classic sigh of a deadly kind
I'm here, but they see me little

I've heard that when all hope seems lost
There's new hope to be found
Since I know by Whose hands I'm made
I'm meant to be around

"Are not five sparrows sold for two pennies?
Yet not one of them is forgotten by God.
Indeed, the very hairs of your head are all numbered.
Don't be afraid; you are worth more than many sparrows."
~ Luke 12:6-7

Sunrise

The quiet of morning
The soft song of a bird
The pink of the sunrise
before life is stirred

Must be like
when the world began
All things were new
yet all things were planned

"Now the earth was formless and empty,
darkness was over the surface of the deep,
and the Spirit of God was hovering over the waters."
~ Genesis 1:2

Mighty God

Did God give us the sun
to remind us of Him . . .
To show us what we're in for
when earth's light starts to dim?

"Lord, our Lord, how majestic is your name in all the earth!"
~ Psalm 8:9

36

His Care In All Things

When an ant carries
When wind moves the leaves
When palm branches creak
and when birds nest in trees

When pine needles fall
When stars, they sit right
When sunrise, it beams
And moon claims the night

When a creature is born
or yet, born and made new
From a worm to a butterfly
wings, purple and blue

It's these things . . .
All these things remind me of You
And the care that You take
in all things that You do

*"The whole earth is filled with awe at your wonders;
where morning dawns, where evening fades,
you call forth songs of joy."*
~ Psalm 65:8

Earth And Sky

Well, I am just a man
loved by the One Who
made the earth and sand
and gave the sky its blue

I don't understand
Your every reason why
But mine is not to know
And Yours is earth and sky

"*The heavens declare the glory of God;
the skies proclaim the work of his hands.*"
~ Psalms 19:1

Gold

The sun, moon, and stars
tell a story
The birds, trees, and sea
tell His glory
I know that He lives
'cause the life that He gives
Remember before
when all was a haze?
When seeing was walking
in being afraid?
And the fog only lifted
when moments away
From what could've been all
at the end of the day?
Looking back, I can see
that He followed me through
The tunnels that lead
to the depths of the blue
Down dark, winding roads
under earth, out of view
'Til my feet could find place

in the land that He knew
I've never a spot I can go,
out of reach ~
Where His voice cannot fill
where His eyes cannot see
Where His ears do not hear
the wee cry of one me,
For when falling, prayers rise
to the Father that Be
He Is, I Am
the One Who holds
The One Who searches
wandering folds
The One Who loves
when all seems cold
The One Who gave
the clay, the Gold

*"By faith we understand that the universe
was formed at God's command, so that what is seen
was not made out of what was visible."*
~ Hebrews 11:3

That Is Why He Came

I was planted in the heart of a Savior
with lots to do when He came
Souls to save, bodies to heal
and human pride to tame

I was planted in the heart of a Savior
with nothing else on His mind
but the Father's heart, the Father's love
the apple of His eye

I was planted in the heart of a Savior
Who would never forget my name
He lived to die, so I'd die to live
For, that is why He came

"But God demonstrates his own love for us in this:
While we were still sinners, Christ died for us."
~ Romans 5:8

The Greatest Love Story Ever Told

Your heart, broken for me
Your wounds, felt for me
Your body, bent for me
Your death, for me
My sin, placed upon You
Those thorns, embedded into You
The taunts, thrown up at You
The blood, drained from You
The love, given to me
The love, showered on me
The love, stored up for me
The cross, carried for me
The breath, taken for me
The sting of a whip, endured for me
The sorrow, for me
The sadness, for me
The flesh, torn for me

The searching, for me
The healing, for me
The story, for me
The truth, for me
The grace, for me
The mercy, for me
The best . . . for me
The greatest love story ever told

" . . . he bore the sin of many . . . "
~ Isaiah 53:12

She Opened Her Eyes

While a tear runs down her frail face
I can see the years flood through
She loves the man that you've become
and the boy she sees in you

She opened her eyes and I saw light
I've never seen before tonight
She lifted her head and I fell back
Oh, that kind of love

The years move fast, and slow us down
Pain, to both body and soul
But the promises of God are sound
He will lead us home

While a tear runs down her frail face
I can see the years flood through
No wishes and no could-have-beens
Just the love she has for you

"My command is this: Love each other as I have loved you."
~ John 15:12

I AM

If you walk into dark places
Know that I Am

If you feel the wind knocked clean out of you
Know that I Am

If you are overcome with grief
Know that I Am

"I, even I, am he who comforts you."
~ Isaiah 51:12

A Thousand Stars

You take my hand
and walk with me
I can't help but
look at your feet
They said the nails,
they ran so deep . . .

I look into your eyes,
and you say,

"You are worth a thousand stars,
and all the birds in the sky . . .
and all the fish in the sea . . .
Yes, I remember the storm,
but you were worth it to Me"

"For God so loved the world that he gave his one and
only Son, that whoever believes in him shall not
perish but have eternal life."
~ John 3:16

The
Beginning